The First Book of Printing

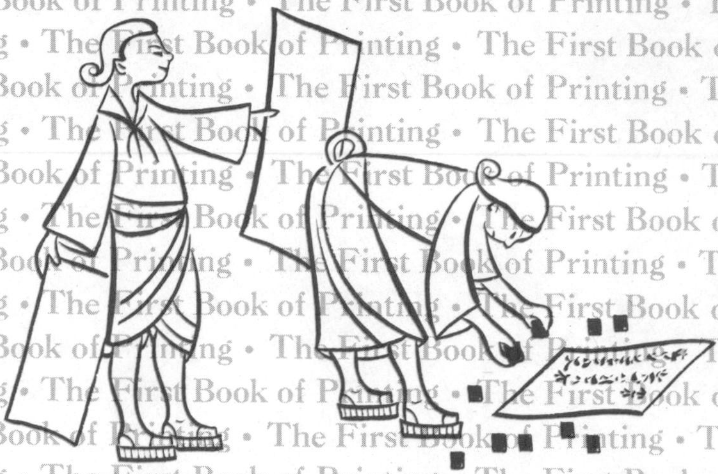

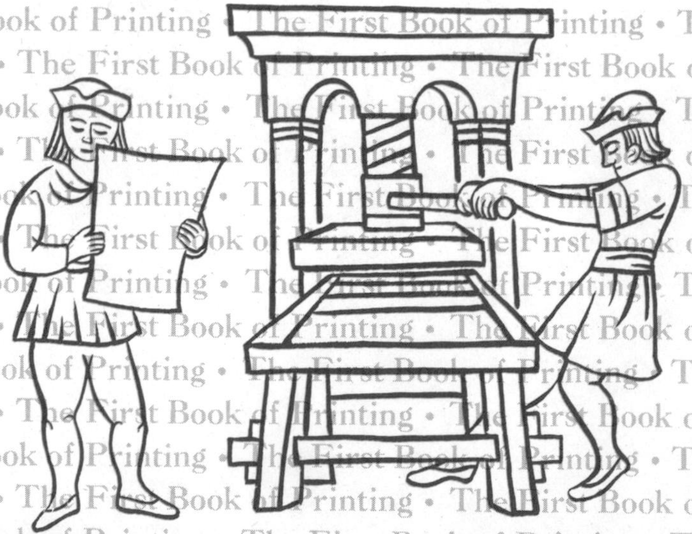

Book of Printing • The First Book of Printing • The First Book of Printing • The Fir
ting • The First Book of Printing • The First Book of Printing • The First Book of
Book of Printing • The First Book of Printing • The First Book of Printing • The Fir
ting • The First Book of Printing • The First Book of Printing • The First Book of Pri
Book of Printing • The First Book of Printing • The First Book of Printing • The Fir
ting • The First Book of Printing • The First Book of Printing • The First Book of Pri
Book of Printing • The First Book of Printing • The First Book of Printing • The Fir
ting • The First Book of Printing • The First Book of Printing • The First Book of Pri
Book of Printing • The First Book of Printing • The First Book of Printing • The Fir
ting • The First Book of Printing • The First Book of Printing • The First Book of Pri
Book of Printing • The First Book of Printing • The First Book of Printing • The Fir
ting • The First Book of Printing • The First Book of Printing • The First Book of Pri
Book of Printing • The First Book of Printing • The First Book of Printing • The Fir
ting • The First Book of Printing • The First Book of Printing • The First Book of Pri
Book of Printing • The First Book of Printing • The First Book of Printing • The Fir
ting • The First Book of Printing • The First Book of Printing • The First Book of Pri
Book of Printing • The First Book of Printing • The First Book of Printing • The Fir
ting • The First Book of Printing • The First Book of Printing • The First Book of Pri
Book of Printing • The First Book of Printing • The First Book of Printing • The Fir
ting • The First Book of Printing • The First Book of Printing • The First Book of Pri
Book of Printing • The First Book of Printing • The First Book of Printing • The Fir
ting • The First Book of Printing • The First Book of Printing • The First Book of Pri
Book of Printing • The First Book of Printing • The First Book of Printing • The Fir
ting • The First Book of Printing • The First Book of Printing • The First Book of Pri
Book of Printing • The First Book of Printing • The First Book of Printing • The Fir
ting • The First Book of Printing • The First Book of Printing • The First Book of Pri
Book of Printing • The First Book of Printing • The First Book of Printing • The Fir
ting • The First Book of Printing • The First Book of Printing • The First Book of Pri
Book of Printing • The First Book of Printing • The First Book of Printing • The Fir
ting • The First Book of Printing • The First Book of Printing • The First Book of Pri
Book of Printing • The First Book of Printing • The First Book of Printing • The Fir
ting • The First Book of Printing • The First Book of Printing • The First Book of Pri
Book of Printing • The First Book of Printing • The First Book of Printing • The Fir
ting • The First Book of Printing • The First Book of Printing • The First Book of Pri
Book of Printing • The First Book of Printing • The First Book of Printing • The Fir
ting • The First Book of Printing • The First Book of Printing • The First Book of Pri
Book of Printing • The First Book of Printing • The First Book of Printing • The Fir
ting • The First Book of Printing • The First Book of Printing • The First Book of Pri

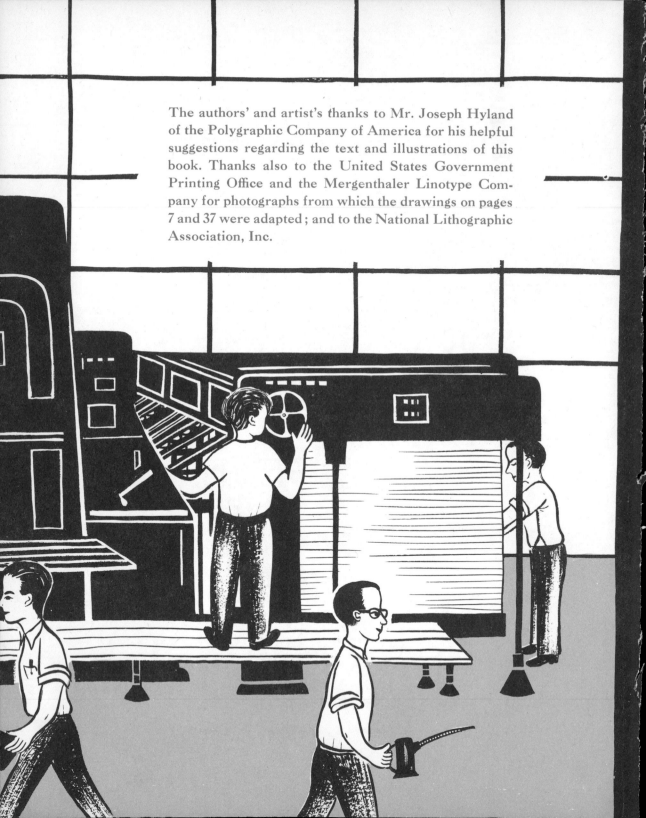

The authors' and artist's thanks to Mr. Joseph Hyland of the Polygraphic Company of America for his helpful suggestions regarding the text and illustrations of this book. Thanks also to the United States Government Printing Office and the Mergenthaler Linotype Company for photographs from which the drawings on pages 7 and 37 were adapted; and to the National Lithographic Association, Inc.

The FIRST BOOK of
PRINTING

by

SAM and BERYL EPSTEIN

Pictures by LÁSZLO ROTH

FRANKLIN WATTS, INC.
575 LEXINGTON AVENUE
NEW YORK 22, N. Y.

Copyright 1955 by Franklin Watts, Inc.

6 7 8

Type set by Kurt H. Volk, Inc.
Printed by Offset Lithography in the United States of America
by the Polygraphic Company of America, Inc.
Bound by H. Wolff Book Manufacturing Co., Inc.

Library of Congress Catalog Number: 55-9601

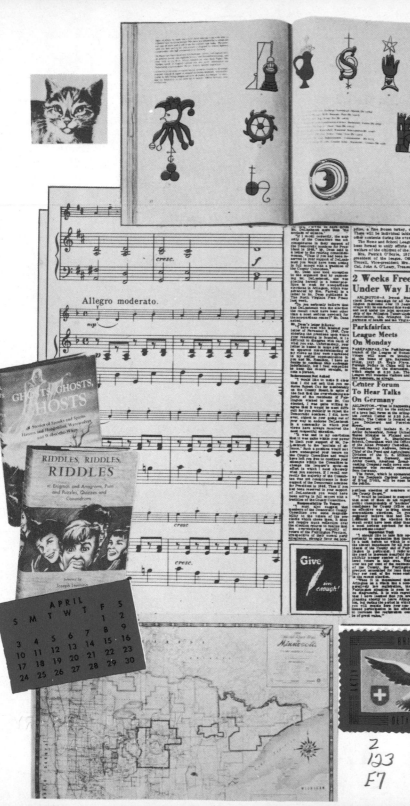

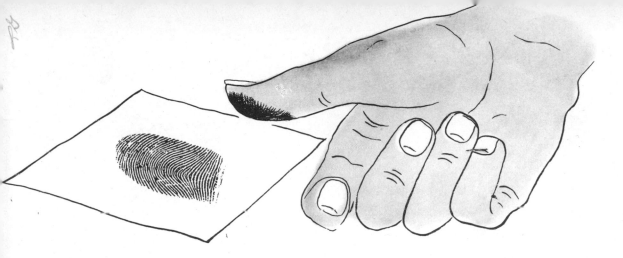

Your own printing press

Everyone in the world has his own printing press right at his fingertips.

If you press the ball of your thumb on an ordinary ink pad, and then press it on a sheet of paper, you will make a fingerprint. The design of your thumb will be printed on the paper by the same method a printer uses to print words or pictures on the pages of a book.

If you ink your thumb a second time, and press it once more on the paper, you will make an exact duplicate of the first thumbprint. This will prove that printing is simply the process of making a number of identical copies of any design or pattern.

Your fingerprint is a good example of the kind of printing called **relief printing**, and if you look closely at your thumb you will understand how it works. The pattern on your thumb is made up of tiny ridges, or hills, and valleys. The ridges stand out "in relief." When you press your thumb on the ink pad, the tops of those ridges get black. And when you press your thumb on the paper, you print the pattern made by the ridges.

1

There is another method of printing which is the opposite of relief printing. It is called **intaglio printing** (pronounced in-TAL-yoh), from the Italian word *tagliare*, which means "to carve." An intaglio design is a design that has been cut or carved into a surface.

The deep lines on your thumb, for example, that form tiny valleys or grooves between the ridges, make an intaglio design. If you get a great deal of ink on your thumb, and then wipe most of it off so that the tops of the ridges are clean and ink is left only in the grooves, you can make a fingerprint by the intaglio method.

This will be the exact opposite of a fingerprint made by the relief method. The relief print will show the pattern of the high ridges on your finger. The intaglio print will show the pattern of the low grooves. Every place that is dark on one print will be light on the other.

There is a third method of printing, and this one doesn't depend either on ridges or on grooves. It is called **surface** or **planographic printing**. Planographic comes from the Greek words which mean

Paul Andrew   *werbnA luaP*

"flat writing," and it is done with a perfectly smooth surface.

If you write your name in ink on a smooth sheet of paper, and then press another sheet of paper on top of it before the ink is dry, you will pick up the inked letters on the second sheet. That sheet will now be printed by the surface method.

But look carefully at the printed name. It is backward! This shows you one important thing about *all* printing: every printed sheet is a backward image of the original. If you want to print your name so that it reads correctly, you have to write it backwards in the first place. Then, when you press a sheet of paper over your name, the paper will pick up a backward image of the backward letters.

When this page was printed all the lines were backward in the printing press so that they would read correctly when they were printed.

Each of these three methods—relief, intaglio, and surface can be used to print both words and pictures. They are the three most important printing methods ever invented, and they are used today to print thousands of things.

3

A printed newspaper brings you the news of the whole wide world. The mailman brings you printed postcards and printed announcements of sales or important meetings. Printed bus or train tickets take you to school or to your job. Your milk and cereal and lots of other foods come in printed containers that tell exactly what is inside them.

Printed labels show the brand name of the toys and tools you buy, and printed directions tell how to use them. You turn to printed books when you want to be entertained or to learn something — whether it is how to be an engineer or how to bake a cake, the number of a friend's telephone, the date of a famous battle, or the right way to pronounce a word. Printed magazines bring you stories and cartoons and all sorts of interesting information.

Printed paper money is handier to carry around than heavy coins made of metal. Printed checks are useful for paying the household bills, and it is easier to mail the checks, using printed stamps to pay for the service, than to deliver them in person.

All day, every day, you live and think the way you do because you have printed things to help you. It is hard to imagine what the world would be like if nothing had ever been printed at all.

The seals of ancient kings

Printing as we know it today, done on giant machines that can turn out thousands of printed sheets in a single hour, is quite a recent invention. But the idea of printing — of making many copies or impressions of a single thing — is very, very old.

Thousands of years ago the king of Babylonia had a smooth stone or jewel carved with a special design that was his own mark — what we might call his signature. This stone was known as a seal. When he pressed the seal into a damp clay tablet, on which a new law had just been carved, he was printing his signature on it and making it official.

Many people today still wear seal rings, or signet rings, with their names or initials carved on them. These rings too can be used to print the carved letters in soft wax or some other soft substance.

More than 4,000 men and women work for the New York *Times,* one of the world's biggest newspapers, which is printed in a 14-story building in the heart of New York City. Every day 1,000,000 words of news pour into this building from all over the world, by telephone, telegraph, radio, and radio-telephone. More than 150 reporters bring in the news of events that happen in New York City alone. Skillful editors cut this huge amount of news down to the 145,000 words that will be printed each day, and other experts write the headlines that will be printed at the top of each story. Pictures to be printed in the paper are brought in by *Times* photographers, or received from distant places by car, train, wire, wireless, or telephone. The paper's big presses can each print 16 pages at a time, and can turn out 400,000 news-papers, folded and ready for delivery, in a single hour. A daily edition of the *Times* may have from 48 to 64 pages, and a Sunday edition may have as many as 360 pages.

BIGGEST PRINTING JOBS

The huge Government Printing Office in Washington, D.C., one of the largest and best-equipped printing plants in the world, has over 7,000 employees and uses more than 62,000 tons of paper a year. Every year it prints over 4,000,000 copies of the *Congressional Record,* the daily report of everything that goes on in Congress. It also prints millions of copies each year of the 50,000 books, pamphlets, and other publications issued by the United States Government, and about 2,500,000,000 postal cards.

The first real printers

The Chinese were probably the real inventors of printing because they were the first to use carved stones for making copies of something more than a man's mark or his signature. Many hundreds of years ago the Chinese discovered how to print a whole new law, or some other piece of writing, all at once. They carved the law on a stone, sprinkled a kind of sooty dust over the carving, and then put a piece of paper over it and rubbed the paper until the sooty lines came off on its underside.

A Japanese empress used this Chinese method when she wished to tell all her people about the Buddhist religion. She ordered an

8

artist to carve a Buddhist saying, or text, on a block of wood. Then the artist put ink on the block and used it to print the text on hundreds of small pieces of paper. Some of those pieces of paper printed at the command of the empress have been preserved to this day. They are 1,200 years old, the oldest pieces of printed paper known to exist.

Printing done with a carved block, which is called block printing, was the only kind of printing known for many centuries. It is still used today for certain kinds of pictures. For example, many people make their own linoleum cuts — sheets of ordinary linoleum into which a design has been carved — and use them to print cards or posters. But block printing is not often used today for the printing of words, because it is such a slow process.

Every time an ancient king wanted to have a new law printed by this method, his printer had to carve the whole law, letter by letter and word by word, on a block of wood or a clay tablet. If the king put the same words at the beginning of each new law, words like "I decree this law unto all my people," the printer had to carve those words over again each time. And each carefully carved block had to be thrown away after the new law was printed, because it was useless for printing anything else.

Finally, about 800 years ago, a Chinese printer named Pi Sheng had a clever idea. Instead of carving a whole new law on a single big block of wood or a single clay tablet, he made each Chinese word or character separately out of a bit of clay. By fitting the proper clay pieces together in rows in a kind of box the way small children fit their blocks together to spell out words,

9

he could print the new law just as he always did. But when he was finished he could keep all the separate pieces of clay and use them over again whenever he wanted to. He could fit them together in a new way to form the sentences of another law.

Those little pieces of clay are called pieces of type, and Pi Sheng had invented something important. He had invented movable type — individual pieces of type that could be recombined to form new and different sentences. A little later even better movable type was made out of wood.

A Korean printer made the next improvement. After he arranged all his pieces of type in a box called a **form** so that they spelled out what he wanted to print, he pressed the form against fine wet sand. Each piece of type made a little impression or mold in the sand. Then he heated some metal until it melted and poured it over the sand, letting it fill up all the letter-shaped molds. When the metal cooled it hardened into a solid plate with raised images

10

of the letters on the underside. He could use the metal sheet for printing on paper.

The metal sheet was much easier to work with than a box of small pieces of type. And, besides, while the metal sheet was being used to print one page, the separate pieces of type could be put together in a new way to make another metal sheet which would print another page. The Korean printer had invented the **type mold**, which is still used today.

For more than a hundred years, from about the year 1300, the Koreans were the best printers in the world. Their ruler was so pleased with this new invention that he formed a government department of printing. It published many copies of the country's laws and stories, and Korea became the first country in the world where ordinary people could afford to own copies of such things.

11.

Europe wanted books too

But Europe and the rest of the western world didn't hear about the new printing methods invented in China and Korea. Europe had been living through a long period sometimes called the Dark Ages, when few people knew how to read and few people cared about learning new things. The Dark Ages began in about the year 476, when rough and warlike tribes from Germany and other northern lands destroyed the city of Rome, in Italy, then the most civilized city in the western world.

Rome had not known the art of printing, but she had many books that had been carefully written out by hand — some in the ancient Greek language and some in Rome's own language, Latin. When the city fell most of those hand-written books were destroyed. Only a few were saved by scholars who carried them away secretly to Turkey and other lands in the East. And for many hundreds of years afterward there were almost no books in Europe at all.

12

Then a few of the scholars, mostly priests of the Christian Church, began to make their way into Europe. They brought hand-written books with them. In the monasteries specially trained priests called scribes copied out word for word the few precious books the scholars had brought.

The scribes wrote carefully and the books they made were often beautiful. Tiny pictures painted in scarlet, blue, and green against a background of real gold filled the edges of almost every page and surrounded the first letter of each new paragraph. The pictures were so bright that they were called **illuminations**. But each hand-written illuminated book took many long months of skilled and careful labor. When it was finished it was hidden away like a precious jewel. Only noblemen were wealthy enough to buy such a costly work of art. So priests and noblemen were the only ones who ever saw books in those days.

Most of the people of Europe at that time were peasants. They lived like slaves, working on the land the noblemen owned. There was no way a peasant could get any money for himself, because he wasn't paid for his work. And there was no way he could get an education except by listening to the talk of his father and other older men, and learning the things they knew about planting crops and tending cattle. Each peasant had to live the same hard life his father had lived, in poverty and ignorance.

But finally the peasants revolted and seized some of their rulers' land for themselves. And then they wanted knowledge, too, so that they would know how to use their new possessions and their new freedom. They began to demand books — hundreds of books, thousands of books, so that each man could have his own and could learn to read them for himself.

That's how it happened that here and there in Europe, beginning in about the year 1400, a few men began to seek some new method of making books that would be quicker than writing out each book by hand.

They didn't know about the printing methods used in China. But they began to discover the art of printing for themselves.

Some of them used carved wooden blocks, like the ones the Chinese had used before they invented movable type. But of course block-printing was very slow and costly, and they used it mostly for printing a picture, or a picture and a few words, on a single sheet of paper. Once in a while they fastened several of those sheets together to make a little booklet, but they couldn't print such booklets fast enough or cheaply enough to meet the great new demand for books.

15

Johann Gutenberg and his type

Nobody is really sure which pioneering European printer finally invented movable type and worked out a satisfactory method of making and using it. Probably several men had some good ideas at about the same time, and slowly the ideas were put together.

Perhaps the first man who successfully used movable type was a Dutchman named Laurens Janszoon, who was a sexton or Koster in the town of Haarlem, and who is sometimes called Laurens Koster.

But more probably it was a German known as Johann Gutenberg, who was born in the town of Mainz in about the year 1397. Johann's real name was Gensfleisch, which means Goose Flesh. Apparently he didn't like it very well, because he always called himself by his mother's name, Gutenberg, which means Good Mountain.

Gutenberg borrowed money to experiment with certain new "tools," as he called them. Experts believe that those "tools" may have been the first satisfactory movable metal type in Europe.

Probably Gutenberg hired a skilled metalworker to cut each letter of the alphabet in relief on the end of a small stick, or punch. This punch was then used to press the shape of each letter into a small square of metal. The letter-shaped hollow made by the punch was what printers called a **matrix**. When Gutenberg had a matrix for each letter of the alphabet, he could make his type, making A's from the A matrix, B's from the B matrix and so on.

In order to make pieces of type of the letter A he fitted four pieces of wood around the A matrix in such a way that the matrix formed the bottom of a tiny open box. If he looked down into the

17

box he could see the shape of the letter A hollowed out on the floor. At the top of the box was a funnel.

Gutenberg poured hot melted metal through the funnel into the box, first letting it fill up the letter-shaped mold at the bottom and then pouring in more metal until the box was filled right to the top. After the metal cooled and hardened, he removed the sides of the box and picked up the metal. It was in the shape of a tiny block with the letter A in relief on its underside.

Afterward Gutenberg could put the box back together again and cast several more pieces of type of the letter A. And when he had made as many A's as he needed, he could rebuild the little box, this time around the B matrix, and cast as many pieces of type of B as he needed.

The movable walls of the little box in which Gutenberg made his type formed a mold that is called an **adjustable type mold**, because it could be adjusted to fit all letters. The invention of this mold was an important step forward in the development of a quicker and cheaper method of printing.

Gutenberg discovered that the best metal to use for his type was a mixture of lead and tin and antimony. This metal didn't shrink when it cooled, so he could be sure that all his letters would be exactly like the original matrix, and that his pieces of type would fit neatly together in snug rows. This mixture of lead and tin and antimony is still used for the making of type today. It is called **type metal**.

The famous Gutenberg Bible

Gutenberg never put his own name on anything he printed, and that's why nobody can be sure about the printing he did. But experts think that his first important book, and probably the first important book printed with movable type in all of Europe, was a big Bible now usually called the Gutenberg Bible, finished in about the year 1456.

There are still several copies of this famous book in existence. One is in the New York Public Library in New York City. Not long ago one copy of this book was sold for more than one hundred thousand dollars.

The Gutenberg Bible is printed in Latin, with two columns of type, each 42 lines long, on every page. It fills 1,282 pages. For each of those pages Gutenberg had to arrange his type in rows, ink it, and press paper down on it in his printing press. Probably his press was an old wine press, with a heavy screw that had to be lowered to press the paper against the type, and then raised so that the printed sheet could be removed, the type inked again, and a fresh sheet of paper put on it.

Gutenberg printed 200 copies of this Bible, which means that he had to ink and print each page of type 200 times. And when each page had been printed, he had to sort his pieces of type and rearrange them to spell out the words of the next page. The printing of the Bible probably took about five years.

If you look at a page of the Gutenberg Bible you can learn a good deal about early printing.

The first thing you notice is that all the large letters, or capitals, are in red, and that some of them are decorated. These letters were not printed when the rest of the page was on the press. They were added later, painted or written in by hand. And the decorations at the top and bottom of the page were hand painted too.

These hand-painted letters and illuminations, and the shape of the printed letters themselves, show that an early printer wanted his book to look like the valuable handwritten books of that time. Each printed letter was made to look as much as possible like a handwritten letter. Early printing, in other words, was an imitation of hand-printing, and even today most of the styles of type that printers use were originally designed to look like the hand-

obsedit me. Foderūt manus meas
et pedes meos: dinumerauerūt oīa
ossa mea. Ipsi vero cōsiderauerunt
et inspexerūt me: diuiserūt sibi vesti-
menta mea: et sup veste mea miserūt
sortem. Tu aut dūe ne elongaueris
auxiliū tuū: ad defensionē mea ōspice.
Erue a framea deus animā meam:
et de manu canis unicā meam. Sal-
ua me ex ore leonis: et a cornibz uni-
corniū humilitatē mea. Narrabo nomen tuū fratribz meis: in medio eccle-
sie laudabo te. Qui timetis dūm lau-
date eū: uniūsū seme iacob glorifica-
te eū. Timeat eū oīe seme israhel:
quonia nō spreuit neqz despexit depre-
rationē pauperis. Nec auertit faciem
suā a me: et cū clamarē ad eū exaudi-
uit me. Aput te laus mea in ecclesia
magna: vota mea reddā in cōspectu
timetiū eū. Edent pauperes et satura-
buntur: et laudabūt dūm qui requirūt
eū: viuet corda eoq in sclin seculi. Re-
miniscentur et conuertentur ad dūm:
uniūsi fines terre. Et adorabunt in
cōspectu eiº: uniūse familie gentium.
Quonia dūi est regnū: et ipse dūabi-
tur gentiū. Manducauerūt et adora-
uerūt oīes pingues terre: in cōspectu
eius cadet omnes qui descendūt in ter-
ram. Et anima mea illi viuet: et se-
men meū seruiet ipi. Annunciabitur
dūo generatio ventura: et annuncia-
bunt celi iusticiā eiº ipso qui nascetur
quē fecit dominus. psalmº dauid XXII
Dominº regit me et nichil michi
deerit: in loco pascue ibi me col-
locauit. Super aquā refectionis edu-
cauit me: animā mea cōuertit. De-
duxit me super semitas iusticie: ppter
nomen suū. Nam et si ambulauero
in medio vmbre mortis non timebo

mala: quonia tu mecum es. Virga
tua et baculus tuus: ipa me cōsolata
sunt. Parasti in cōspectu meo mesā:
aduersus eos qui tribulāt me. Impin-
guasti in oleo caput meū: et calix meus inebrias quā pclarus est. Et mi-
sericordia tua subsequetur me: omnibz
diebz vite mee. Et ut inhabitem i do-
mo domini: in longitudinē dierum.
Psalmº dauid in pīa sabbati. XXIII
Domini est terra et plenitudo eiº:
orbis terraq et uniuersi qui habi-
tant in eo. Quia ipse sup maria fuu-
dauit eū: et super flumina preparauit
eū. Quis ascendit i montem dūi: aut
quis stabit in loco sancto eiº. Inno-
cens manibz et mūdo corde: qui non
accepit in vano animā suā: nec iura-
uit in dolo proximo suo. Hic accipi-
et benedictionē a dūo: et misericordiā
a deo salutari suo. Hec est generatio
querentiū eū: querentiū facie dei iacob.
Attollite portas principes vestras
et eleuamini porte eternales: et introibit rex glorie. Quis est iste rex glorie.
dūs fortis et potens: dominº potens in
prelio. Attollite portas principes vestras et eleuamini porte eternales: et
introibit rex glorie. Quis est iste rex
glorie. dominus virtutum ipse est
rex glorie. In fine psalmº dauid XXIIII
Ad te dūe leuaui animā mea: deus meus i te confido nō erubesca. Neqz
irrideant me inimici mei: etenim uniuersi qui sustinēt te nō confundentur.
Confundātur omnes iniqua agen-
tes: super vacue. Vias tuas domine
demonstra michi: et semitas tuas edo-
ce me. Dirige me in veritate tua et do-
ce me: quia tu es deus saluator meº:
et te sustinui tota die. Reminiscere
miseracionū tuarum dūe: et misdiaq

writing popular among the book-copiers of certain countries. The type in the Gutenberg Bible, made with heavy black lines in the style of hand lettering popular in Germany in those days, is sometimes called **black letter** because it made a printed page look so black.

One more important thing about this page is that it looks as if it had been designed by an artist. There are nice wide margins. The lines of printing are close together in order to get many words on one page. But if you look at them from a little distance the printed words and the red capital letters make a pleasant pattern. The page doesn't seem ugly or crowded. This is because even the earliest printer, just like the printer of today, wanted every page to look like a well-planned design, so that people would enjoy looking at it even before they read a single word.

More books

When Gutenberg couldn't pay back money he owed to a goldsmith named Johann Fust, he had to give Fust his "tools" instead. So Fust and his son-in-law, Peter Schoeffer, began to print books too. One of their books has a date printed on it, the year 1457. It is the first dated book printed in Europe.

Gutenberg died a poor man, but people in other countries had heard of his printing "tools" and came to Mainz to learn how to make and use movable type. Then they returned to their own lands, to set up printing presses in Italy, Switzerland, France, Holland, Belgium, Spain, and England. They began to print books of all kinds in many languages. They were beginning to supply the thousands of books people had been asking for.

In the year 1450 there were only a few people in all of Europe who had ever seen a printed page. But by the time Columbus discovered America, in 1492, printed books could be found in almost every country. About 40,000 different books had been printed in Europe by then, and there were hundreds of copies of each one, adding up to a total of about 20 million books. All over Europe people's lives began to change because they could read books and learn things their fathers had never had a chance to learn.

N̄VNC Autem teſtimonia etiam exteriorum de ipſis diligenter citabimus. Illuſtriſſimi enim etiā græcorū nō imperiti omnino iudaicæ philoſophiæ alii uitam eorū ſcriptis ſuis approbaſſe uidentur: alii theologiā quantū potuere ſecuti ſūt. Sic eīm diſces nō temere ſed abſoluta exquiſitaq; ratione iudaicā philoſophiā gentilibus nugis præpoſitam a nobis fuiſſe. Primum igit' ea ponā quæ de uita iudæorū præclariſſimi græcorum teſtantur. Theophraſtum igitur audias: cuius nōnullos textus Porphyrius in his libris poſuit quos de abſtinendo a carnibus cōſcripſit: his uerbis iudæi ad hæc uſq; tēpora Theophraſtus

New type for new books

The names of many early printers are still very well known, because the kind of type those men used is still used today, and is sometimes named after them.

Nicolas Jensen, for example, first a coin-maker in France and then a printer in the Italian city of Venice, used letters that he designed after studying the stone carvings of ancient Rome. But Jensen didn't think printed letters had to look exactly like hand-written ones. He thought the most important thing was to make letters that helped people to read quickly and with pleasure. So he designed clear rounded letters, made partly with rather heavy lines and partly with rather thin lines. The little tails or crooks at the end of certain lines, called **serifs**, gave the letters a graceful finish and helped to tie them together in a row, so that the reader's eye could move smoothly from one to the next. Jensen's letters were so handsome and so easy to read that after a while they

S

24

became more popular than the heavy "black letter" type which Gutenberg had used. Letters of this general kind, called **Roman-style** letters, are still used by printers all over the world today, and some of them are still called Jensen.

A French metal-maker named Claude Garamond was the first man who made a special business of carving letters for printers' type, and today printers still use the beautiful letters he designed. They call them Garamond.

Aldus Manutius of Venice was another famous early printer. He designed a kind of narrow slanting type now called **italic,** in honor of Italy, the country where it was first used. By setting his pages in *italic letters,* like these, Aldus could get many words on one page, and this made it possible for him to print small, cheap books that almost everybody could afford to buy. Thousands of people who had never owned a book before were able to own their own copies of these handsome little pocket-sized volumes.

SATYRA VI.

Debetur monstris, quoties fiat ira nocentem
Hunc sexum, et rabie iecur incendente feruntur
Praecipites, ut saxa iugis abrupta, quibus mons
Subtrahitur, cliuoq; latus pendente recedit.
Illam ego non tulerim, quae computat, et scelus ingens
Sana facit, spectant subeuntem fata marito
Alaesum, et similis si permutatio detur
Morte uiri, cupiant animam seruare catellae.
Occurrent multae tibi Belides, atque Eriphyle,
Mane Clytemnestram nullus non uicus habebit.
Hoc tantum refert, quod Tyndaris illa bipennem
Insulsam, et fatuam leua, dextraq; tenebat,
At nunc res agitur tenui pulmone rubetae,
Sed tamen et ferro, si praegustaret Atrides
Pontica ter uicti cautus medicamina regis.

SATYRA SEPTIMA.

Tspes et ratio studiorum in Caesare tantum,
Solus enim tristes hac tempestate camoenas
Respexit, cum iam celebres, notiq; poetae
Balneolum Gabiis, Romae conducere furnos
Tentarent, nec foedum alii, nec turpe putarent
Praecones fieri, cum desertis Aganippes
Vallibus, exuriens migraret in atria Clio.
Nam si pieria quatrans tibi nullus in arca
Ostendatur, ames nomen, uictumq; Macherae,
Et uendas potius, commissa quod auctio uendit
Stantibus oenophorum, tripodes, armaria, cistas
Halcyonem, Bacchi Thebas, et Terea Faustin.
Hoc satius, quam si dicas sub iudice uidi,

SOME FAMOUS PRINTERS

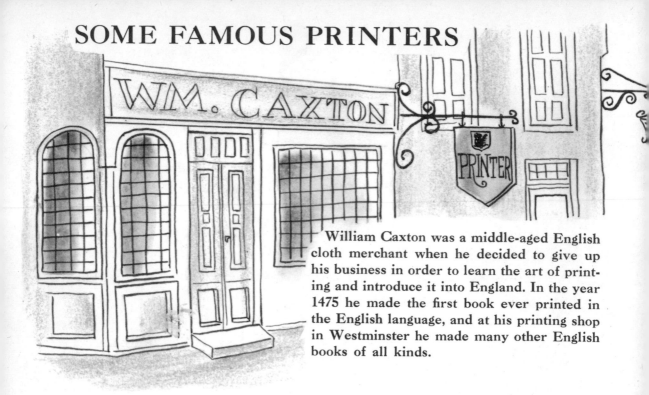

William Caxton was a middle-aged English cloth merchant when he decided to give up his business in order to learn the art of printing and introduce it into England. In the year 1475 he made the first book ever printed in the English language, and at his printing shop in Westminster he made many other English books of all kinds.

Juan Pablo crossed the Atlantic with the Spaniards who conquered Mexico, and set up the first printing press in the New World in 1539 in the city of Mexico. He printed mostly religious textbooks which the Spanish priests used for teaching Christianity to the Indians.

26

The first printing shop in Boston was started by James Franklin, an older brother of Benjamin Franklin, and in 1718 twelve-year-old Benjamin went to work there as an apprentice. Later Benjamin Franklin owned his own printing shop in Philadelphia, where he published his own newspaper and many books, including the famous almanacs he wrote each year called *Poor Richard's Almanacs*.

27

John Peter Zenger came to America from Germany in about 1700. He was put in jail because he attacked the government in his newspaper, the New York *Weekly Journal*. Andrew Hamilton, the lawyer who defended Zenger at his trial, declared that a man should not be arrested for printing what was true. The jury agreed with him and Zenger was freed. This trial helped to establish the idea that every man should be free to print what he believes to be true. Freedom of the press, as this idea is called, became one of the most important principles of American democracy.

AL DVS

Printers' trade-marks

Aldus also designed a sort of trade-mark which he printed at the end of each of his books. It was a little picture of a dolphin, the symbol of speed, twined around an anchor. A printer's trade-mark of this kind is called a **colophon**, which means "finishing stroke." Other printers soon began to use trade-marks, too, and many printers and publishers today have their own colophons.

But nowadays a colophon is not usually found at the end of a book. Instead it is on the title page, the page at the beginning of the book on which the name or title of the book is also printed.

Type styles and sizes

Modern printers use many different kinds of type. This book, for example, is set in the type called Caslon, designed by an Englishman named William Caslon.

Printers also use type of many different sizes, and they measure it in **points**. One point equals 1/72 inch. This sentence is printed in 14-point type.

Here are some examples of type set in different styles and sizes:
This is 14-point type in the style called Garamond.
This is 12-point type in the style called Bodoni.
This is 10-point type in the style called Futura.

Setting type

Gutenberg and other early printers arranged all their type by hand, letter by letter. This process is called **setting type**. There are still printers who set type by hand today. They work standing up, facing the tall cabinet where their type is stored.

This cabinet has many shallow drawers, called **cases**, and each case holds a **font** of type. A font is a complete set of type in some particular style and size, such as 14-point Caslon or 10-point Bodoni. Each font contains many pieces of type of each letter of the alphabet, each number, and each punctuation mark. When a printer decides what font of type he wants to use for a certain job, he pulls out the case containing that font and props it up on top of the cabinet.

Each type case is divided into separate boxes of various sizes. One box holds many small letter a's, one holds many capital A's, one holds question marks, and so on. The boxes are not all the

29

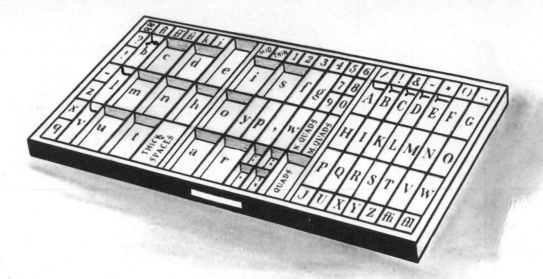

same size, because printers need more types of certain letters and signs than of others. The box for the small letter e is the biggest box of all, because that letter is used more often than any other in the English language and a printer must always have a lot of e's on hand. Other specially big boxes hold the types of other letters that are used very often, such as a, i, t, h and r. The boxes for the most frequently used letters are grouped close together in the middle of the case, so the printer can reach them quickly. This makes it very easy for him to pick out the types he needs for common words like "it" and "the." The boxes that hold the **space bars**—the blank pieces of type used to separate each word from the next one — are also near the center of the case.

Printers used to keep their capital letters in one case and their small letters in another case just below it. Now they keep them all in one case. But they still call their capital letters **upper case** letters and their small letters **lower case** letters.

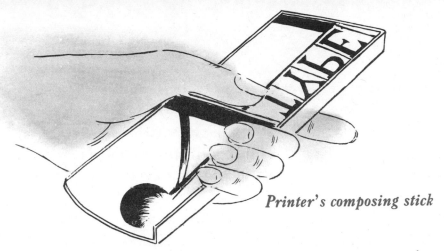

Printer's composing stick

A printer sets type by taking letters from the type case, one by one, and arranging them in rows in a small metal tray called a **stick**, which he holds in his left hand.

Each time he finishes setting one line of type he makes sure it fits snugly into his stick, which he has adjusted to the width of the line he wants. If there is a little space left at the end he slips an extra space bar or two between the words until the line is entirely full. The special space bars he uses for this are so thin that they will not be noticed in the finished printing. Filling out a line of type in this way, so that all his lines will be exactly the same length, is called **justifying** the line.

When the stick is full of neatly justified lines the printer transfers them to a larger metal tray called a **galley**. He may ink each galley of type and print it, to prove that he has not made any mistakes in his typesetting. A paper printed in this way is called a **galley proof**.

When a printer has set enough sticks of type to fill a whole page, he transfers all the rows of type from the galley to a strong metal frame called a **chase**.

31

He is always very careful when he moves lines of type from place to place, because if he drops them all the pieces of type will be mixed up and he will have to sort them out and set them all over again. (Type that has been spilled is called **pied** type.)

When the type is safely in the chase, the printer prepares it for printing. Usually the lines do not take up the whole chase, and so the first thing he must do is fill up the empty space with blocks of wood called **furniture** and wedge-shaped pieces of metal called **quoins**, pronounced coins. This will keep all his lines of type snugly in place, so that no piece of type can fall out or slide out of line. The type locked tightly up is now a **form**.

The last thing he does before he is ready to print is make sure that the whole page of type is exactly level, so that all the letters will print evenly. If one piece of type is lower than the rest it will not reach the paper. And if a few pieces stand up too high, they will hold the paper away from the rest of the type. Usually he evens his type by placing a flat piece of wood on it and tapping the wood lightly with a mallet.

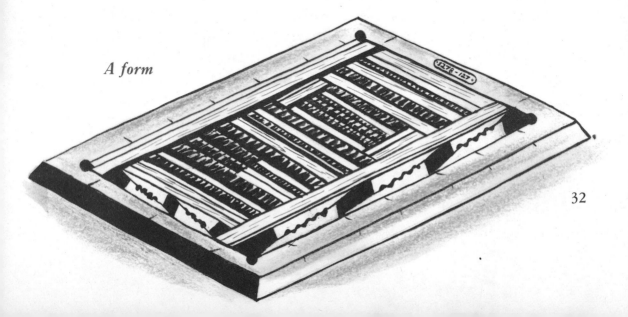

A form

32

The printer's history

An early printer usually had an assistant and perhaps also one of the young apprentices called printer's devils. But sometimes he worked entirely alone, doing everything himself. He might even pack up his metal type and his small hand-operated press and wander from town to town, stopping long enough at each place to do whatever printing jobs were wanted there. And then he wandered on again. He was called a journeyman printer.

A little later there was another kind of wandering printer, and this one carried nothing with him but his skill. In most towns he could easily find a job setting type or running a press, because printing shops were becoming more numerous and busier every year. Printers worked from early morning to late at night, sometimes on books, sometimes on newspapers, sometimes on what they called **job printing**. Job printing is the name given to any small printing job such as a few posters, announcements for a meeting or a farm auction, bill forms for a businessman to send to his customers, or business cards for him to carry in his pocket.

But today there are few printers who work alone and few who wander from place to place. Today most printers work steadily the year round in one place, some in modern job-printing shops, some on newspapers, some in the big printing plants that now turn out the world's books, magazines, catalogues, and other printed material at the rate of thousands of copies an hour.

Printers today learn their trade in special printing schools, and each man is an expert at one of the many different kinds of jobs that are done in every modern printing plant.

This change began to take place when the first printing machines were invented. And those machines were invented because, even with movable type, hand-printing was so slow that it could not satisfy the ever-growing demand for more printed words and pictures.

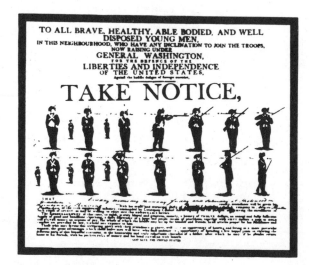

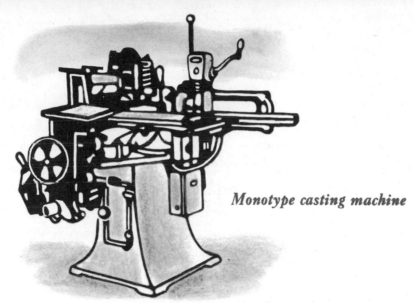

Monotype casting machine

The amazing typesetting machines

The most amazing thing about the typesetting machines is that they don't really set type at all. Instead they **cast** type — mold it fresh from hot liquid metal for each new printing job.

Molding fresh type for each new piece of printing may seem a strange way to speed up the printing process, but it is really much quicker and more efficient than setting already molded type by hand and then putting it back into the type case again when each job is finished. One reason why it is so fast is that freshly molded type doesn't have to be put away after it is used. Instead it is just dumped into a pot and melted down again, to be used over and over in casting new type.

There are two main kinds of type-casting machines. One casts a whole line of type at once and is called the Linotype. The other casts a single letter at a time and is called the Monotype. Both were perfected only after long years of effort, after many people had tried to invent such machines and failed.

The first successful Linotype machine was completed by two Americans, James O. Clephane and Ottmar Mergenthaler, in 1886. Their machine could cast type five times faster than a man could set type by hand. At first the machine's work was not as attractive as hand-set printing, and the Linotype was used only in newspaper offices, where speed was more important than excellent quality. When the Monotype was invented about a dozen years later it was better suited to the printing of fine books, because its single letters could be carefully arranged to make well-designed pages.

But both machines have been improved, and now both are used for all sorts of printing jobs, although the faster Linotype machine is still used by almost all newspapers. Today even an expert usually finds it difficult to tell the difference between type cast by this machine and type set by hand.

The man who operates a typecasting machine is called an operator or a **compositor**. He works sitting down in front of a big keyboard that looks like a big typewriter keyboard. Each key on his board represents one of the letters, numbers, or marks of punctuation that is found in a case of type. Above the keyboard is the frame where he fastens his **copy**, the typewritten newspaper story or magazine article or book manuscript that he is going to set.

As his eyes follow the words of his copy, the Linotype operator's fingers tap it out, letter by letter, on the keyboard. Every time he touches a key a little metal plate drops down into a slot. Each of these plates is really a tiny matrix of a letter like the

36

Linotype machine

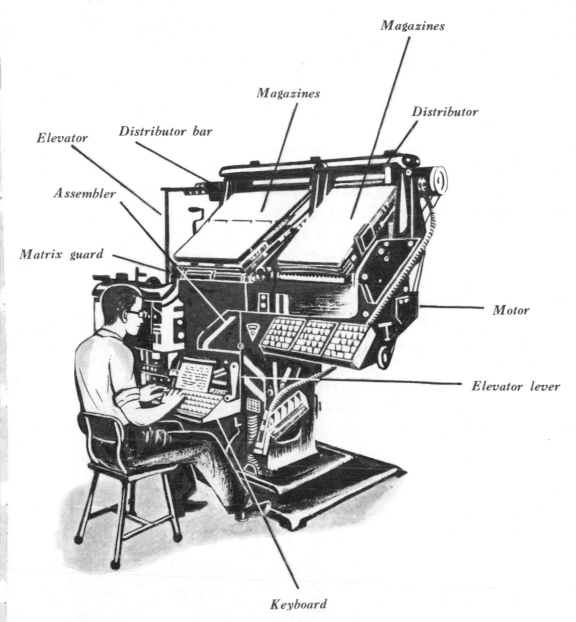

Magazines

Magazines

Distributor

Distributor bar

Elevator

Assembler

Matrix guard

Motor

Elevator lever

Keyboard

matrices from which Gutenberg cast his type by hand. If the operator touches the key marked A, the matrix that drops down will have a capital A carved into its tip. If he touches the keys marked x and 3, the matrices for the small x and the number 3 drop down into the slot.

This slot is called the **assembler**, because it is the place where the matrices assemble, or come together. The operator can see the matrices in the assembler, and if he makes a mistake he can take out the wrong matrix and send the right one down into the slot, putting it in its proper place by hand.

At the end of each word he touches the key that moves two blank wedges into the assembler so that there will be a white space between that word and the next.

When he has spelled out as many words as he can get into the first line, he touches the special key that automatically sends the whole line of matrices to the part of his machine where the mold is located. Here the matrices are automatically justified by widening the spaces between each of the words until the line is entirely filled. Then liquid type metal is forced into the mold from an electrically heated pot so that it fills the hollows in the matrices and forms a metal bar with the whole line of letters in

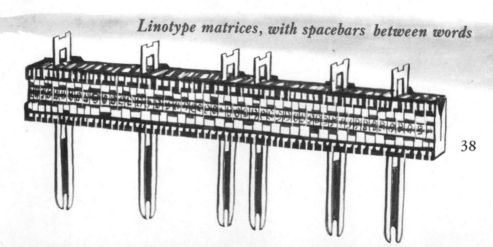

Linotype matrices, with spacebars between words

38

relief on one surface. The machine has now cast a whole line of type.

The newly cast line of type, called a **slug**, then drops down into the galley. Soon it will be joined by another slug and another, until the compositor has finished setting all his copy.

In the meantime, as each line of type drops into the galley, all the matrices that formed that line are carried up to the top of the machine by a piece of machinery something like a tiny elevator. There they travel along a bar called a **distributor bar**. Each matrix has tiny grooves on its underside which fit only into the compartment from which it came. It moves along until it reaches its original place. Then it drops off the bar and is ready for use again.

The operator of a Linotype machine can set type almost as fast as a man can tap out letters on an ordinary typewriter. He can adjust his machine so that it will make lines of many lengths. And he can cast type of almost any style or size by equipping his machine with matrices for the kind of type he wants. Type matrices are kept in flat cases called **magazines**, and a magazine of one font of type can easily be removed from the machine and replaced with a magazine of another font.

Linotype slug

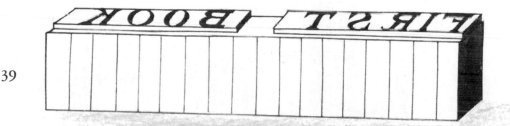

The Monotype is really two machines — a keyboard and a casting machine. The Monotype operator first "keyboards" the copy to be set in type. The "keyboarding," instead of releasing matrices which will cast lines of type, punches holes in a paper ribbon somewhat like the rolls in a player piano. This ribbon is then put on the casting machine, which automatically casts each letter singly as directed by the holes in the ribbon, and pushes the finished lines into a galley.

The Monotype is especially good for setting type to be used in dictionaries and scientific publications that have complicated tables and marks and figures. Corrections can be made by hand without resetting a whole line.

After type is set, it can be printed on a press by any of the three basic printing methods.

Monotype keyboard

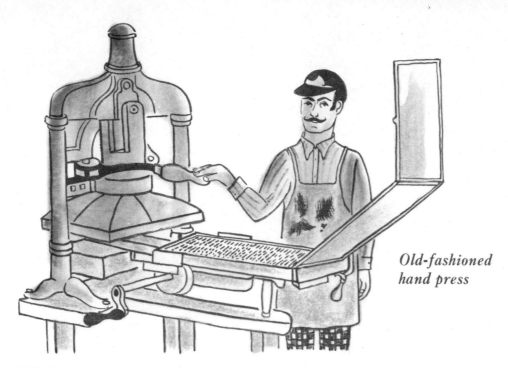

This is a simple press

Every printing press used in a modern printing shop is faster and easier to operate than the press Gutenberg used. Most modern presses, even the smallest ones, run on electric power. But the idea behind all presses is the same. Each one is a machine for pressing paper against inked type.

One of the simplest small modern presses is the one called a platen press. It has three main parts — the **type bed**, the **inking plate**, and the **platen**.

The type bed is the heavy piece of metal to which the type is fastened. In a platen press it stands upright, on its edge, unlike an ordinary bed used in a home. But on some other presses the type bed does lie flat.

41

The inking plate, just above the type bed, is a round metal plate that holds a supply of printer's ink, a greasy substance specially made to stick to metal type. Printers used to daub their ink on the type by hand. But on a modern press the ink is picked up by soft spongy rollers that automatically roll over the inking plate, down over the type, and then up out of the way again, leaving the type freshly inked for the printing of each sheet.

The platen is a heavy flat piece of metal something like the type bed with pins or grippers to hold a sheet of paper in place against it. When the press is in operation fresh sheets of paper feed down onto the platen one at a time. Every time this happens the platen and the type bed come together, face to face, like a pair of hands clapping. This presses the paper against the inked type and prints it. Then the press opens. The platen and the type bed separate again so that the printed sheet may be taken out and a fresh sheet of paper may slide down onto the platen while the type is being inked once more.

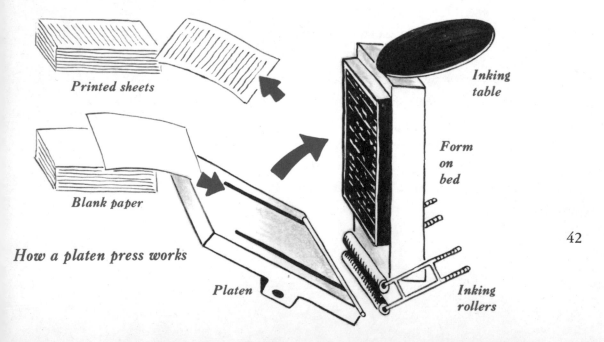

Printed sheets

Blank paper

How a platen press works

Platen

Inking table

Form on bed

Inking rollers

42

Letterpress—printing by the relief method

Newly molded type, fresh from the Linotype machine or the Monotype machine, can be locked into a form and put right on a printing press. But today this is not what usually happens.

In newspaper printing each page of new type is used instead as a mold for making a thick, soft papier maché **mat** — a copy in reverse of that page of type. Then the paper mat is used in turn as a mold for making a metal copy of the whole page. This copy, called a **stereotype**, is a thin sheet of metal with all the type in relief on one side. It is the stereotype that is used for printing.

Book and magazine printers often use a variation of this principle to make plastic plates, rubber plates, or metal plates called electrotypes.

The system of printing from plates or stereotypes instead of printing from type has two important advantages. First, several stereotypes or plates can be made from each original. All metal type wears down and produces blurry print if it is used to print many thousands of copies. This system provides a printer with brand new type at regular intervals, so that all his copies, no matter how many he prints, will be sharp and clear.

Second, the plates or stereotypes can be used on a flat type bed or be bent into a curve to fit around a cylinder.

43

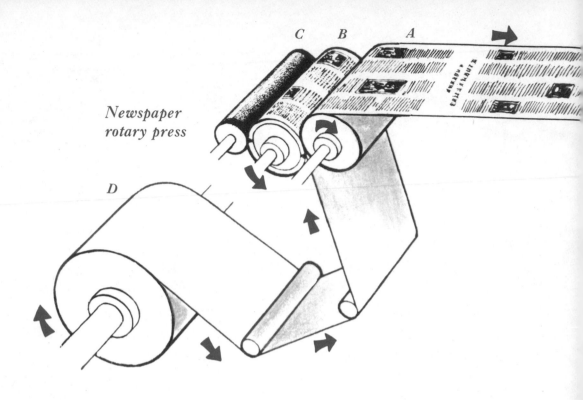

Newspaper rotary press

The big presses

On a big modern newspaper press, called a **rotary press**, the stereotypes are fastened around cylinders. These cylinders keep turning against an endless sheet of moving paper, printing the paper as it goes past. Paper fed into this machine from huge reels can be printed on both sides by automatically inked cylinders and then cut, folded, and bundled so that it comes out of the machine as piles of finished newspapers, ready for delivery.

Cotton cloth and other kinds of cloth are also printed on big machines with cylinders that turn against the cloth and print colored designs on it.

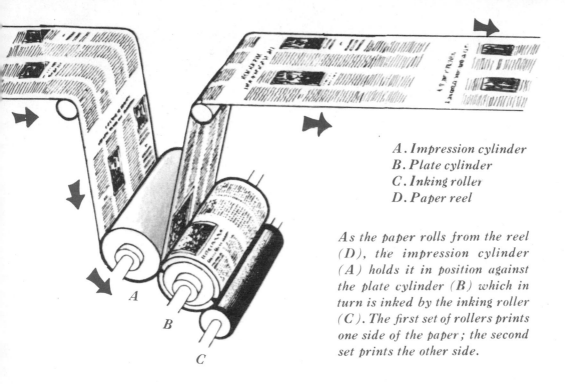

A. Impression cylinder
B. Plate cylinder
C. Inking roller
D. Paper reel

As the paper rolls from the reel (D), the impression cylinder (A) holds it in position against the plate cylinder (B) which in turn is inked by the inking roller (C). The first set of rollers prints one side of the paper; the second set prints the other side.

But flat stereotypes are used on another kind of large press. On this press the type bed is flat, like a table, and slides back and forth beneath a turning cylinder to which the paper is attached. A row of grippers like clutching fingers hold each sheet of paper around the cylinder as it turns against the moving bed of inked type. When the sheet is printed the grippers release it and moving belts carry it away. In the meantime the grippers have picked up another sheet of paper and it is being rolled over the type.

This kind of press, called a **cylinder press,** can print sheets of paper so big that there is room for 32 pages of an ordinary book on each side of the sheet. One of these big sheets, printed on both sides, will make a book of 64 pages.

45

Printing pictures

For a long time all printed pictures were made from carved blocks of wood called woodcuts or wood engravings. The word engrave means to carve.

Then artists discovered that they could engrave pictures on sheets of copper or steel and use these metal sheets for printing. Sometimes they scratched the picture right into the metal with a sharp tool. Sometimes they put a layer of wax on the metal first and made their picture by cutting away the wax in certain places. Then they covered the whole sheet with a kind of acid that dissolves metal but does not dissolve wax. Wherever the wax had been cut away the acid ate into the metal, leaving the wax-covered portions standing up in relief. This process produced a special kind of engraving called an etching.

Metal plates engraved or etched by hand are still used for the printing of pictures today. But now there is also a much faster way to engrave pictures on metal plates. This fast process is done with the help of a camera and is called **photoengraving**. Most of the pictures printed today by letterpress in newspapers, books, and magazines are photoengravings.

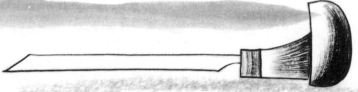

This is how a photoengraving of a cartoon, called a **line cut**, is made:

First the cartoon is photographed, in order to obtain a negative of the drawing on a sheet of transparent film. All the black lines of the original drawing appear light on the negative, and all the white portions appear black. It looks like the ordinary negative a photographer uses for making photographs on paper.

This negative, which is covered with a gelatine-like substance called an emulsion, is used to print the cartoon on a sheet of zinc. The chemicals in the emulsion transfer the cartoon onto the zinc.

Then the zinc is treated with chemicals which eat away the surface of the metal except in the places where the lines of the drawing show on the plate.

The lines of the drawing remain, raised up above the eaten-away surface, and the zinc plate can then be used for printing on paper. The zinc sheet with the photoengraving cut into it is called a line cut because the picture on its surface is formed of simple black lines. Here the cut is mounted on a type-high block of wood, ready for printing.

But not all the pictures used are simple black-and-white cartoons. Some are real photographs, with many shades or tones ranging from solid black through dark gray and light gray to white. In order to print this kind of picture a printer has to make a different kind of photoengraving, called a **halftone engraving.**

The making of a halftone engraving also begins with photographing the original picture, but in this case there is a screen inside the camera which breaks up the picture into thousands of tiny squares. The negative made by this process does not consist of light lines and dark areas. Instead it is made up of thousands of tiny dots, one for each of those squares. And the photoengraving made from this negative also has many tiny dots raised in relief above the eaten-away surface of the metal. The parts of the plate which will print dark patches in the finished picture are covered with fairly large dots that almost or completely touch each other. The parts of the plate that will print gray in the finished picture are covered with smaller dots. The part that will print white patches are covered with dots so tiny that they are almost invisible.

If you look at a printed picture through a magnifying glass you will see that the finished picture also is made up of thousands of tiny dots. Where the dots are big and close together, the picture looks black. Where they are smaller and farther apart the picture looks gray, because your naked eye doesn't see the separate dots. It blurs black dots and white space together to give

48

Part of a halftone screen (enlarged)

you an impression of grayness. Even the parts of the picture that look white to your naked eye are really peppered with black dots, so tiny that you don't see them without a magnifying glass.

There are different kinds of halftone engravings, depending on how fine was the screen used to prepare the plate. Ordinary newspaper pictures are made with screens which produce about 5,000 dots for each square inch of the engraving. A very fine-screened engraving, used for certain expensive books and magazines, has about 18,000 dots in each square inch of its surface.

65-line screen

100-line screen

133-line screen

150-line screen

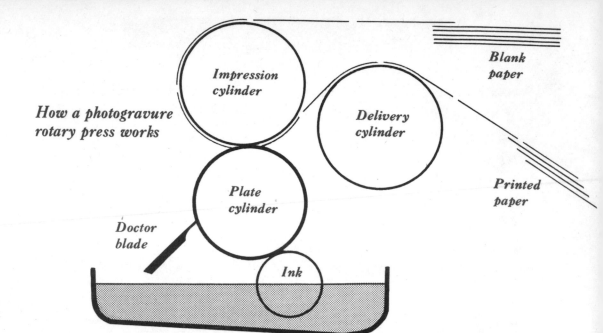

How a photogravure rotary press works

Impression cylinder

Delivery cylinder

Plate cylinder

Doctor blade

Ink

Blank paper

Printed paper

Photogravure: printing by the intaglio method

The printing of pictures and type by the method called photogravure is popular today, especially for magazines.

Photogravure, sometimes called rotogravure when it is done on rotary presses, is a modern form of intaglio printing, with the ink held in the hollows of a plate rather than on the high relief sections. The plate for this kind of printing is made like a halftone plate with the aid of a camera and with acid to eat away certain portions of the metal. The acid forms hollows of different depths, some very shallow and some quite deep. The deep hollows, which hold a lot of ink, will print the type or the darkest areas of the picture. Shallower parts, holding less ink, print more lightly, in various shades of gray depending on each hollow's depth.

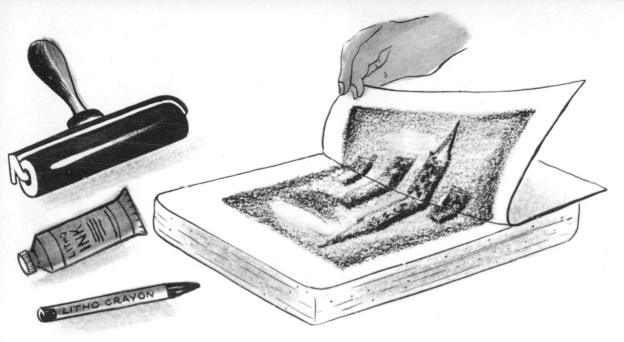

Lithography:
printing by the surface method

There are two kinds of modern lithography, which is a form of surface printing. One is done by hand, by skilled artists. The other called photo-lithography, is done by machine with the aid of a camera. But both kinds of lithography depend on one important fact: oil and water do not mix.

Lithography done by hand is a simple process, but an artist can print beautiful pictures by this method. First he draws his picture on a smooth flat stone with a special kind of oily crayon. Next he rolls a water-soaked roller over the stone. The water clings to the bare stone surface, but it does not stick to the oily crayon marks. Then he rolls the stone with another roller soaked with greasy printer's ink. The ink can't stick to the wet stone because it won't mix with water, but it *can* stick to the oily crayon marks. When the artist presses a sheet of paper against the inked stone, the paper picks up ink only from the places where he drew his lines with the crayon, and in that way he prints his original drawing on the paper.

Photo-lithography, or photo-offset, which is done by machine, uses a zinc plate instead of a smooth stone. The design is put on the plate by a photographic process rather than by hand. The blackened portions of the plate are like the crayon lines on the stone. They can't be wet by water but they can pick up ink. Letters and words can be printed on one of these plates too, but first the words must be set up in type and printed on paper. Then the printing on the paper can be transferred to the zinc plate by photography.

This prepared zinc plate is attached to a printing press by curving it around a cylinder. As the cylinder turns, the plate presses against a roller wet with water and then against an ink roller, so that the blackened portions of the plate are covered

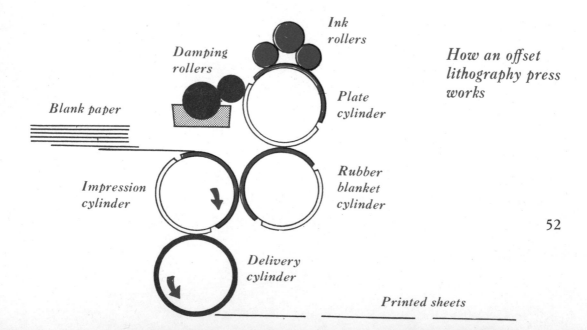

Ink rollers

Damping rollers

Blank paper

Plate cylinder

How an offset lithography press works

Impression cylinder

Rubber blanket cylinder

Delivery cylinder

Printed sheets

with ink. But the newly inked plate doesn't print directly on paper. Instead it rolls against another cylinder covered by a rubber blanket, and the rubber blanket picks up the image. Then the blanket-covered cylinder rolls against a cylinder covered with paper, and the image is transferred or "offset" onto the paper. That's why this kind of printing press is called an offset press, and why this process is called photo-offset printing.

The photo-offset method is becoming more popular every day. Now many books, magazines, and pamphlets are printed in this way. This kind of lithography is also used for the printing of music and for most of the big signs that appear on billboards. It is also used to print big sheets of tin-coated steel, which are then cut up and shaped into the tin cans in which oil, peanuts, soft drinks, and many other products are sold.

53

*A four-color
offset lithography press*

Printing in color

Of course a printer can use ink of any color he likes, although black ink is the most common for the printing of type and for ordinary photographs.

But when a printer wants to print two or more colors at once on a page, regardless of what printing method he uses, he must have a separate plate for each color and must print his page over again with each plate. If he wants to print a page of black type with a red border around it, for example, he needs one plate for the type and another for the border, and must print his page twice.

He uses a special form of this same system to print what are called full-color pictures. These are copies of color photographs, or of paintings, in which every tint of the rainbow appears from darkest purple to palest orange. Probably no printer could afford

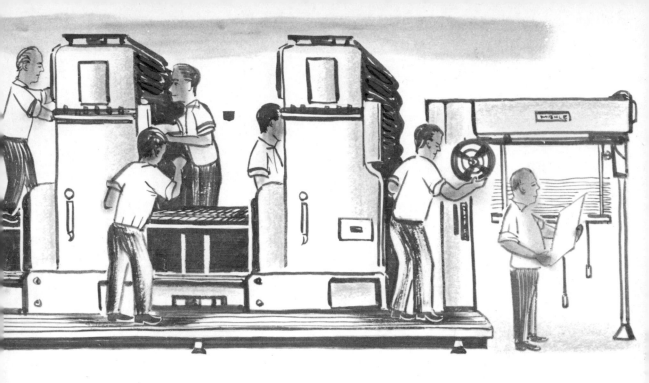

to print full-color pictures if he had to have a plate for every separate shade and tint in that kind of picture. Sometimes printers do use twelve or even more color plates for an especially expensive job. But fortunately most full-color pictures can be printed by a special process with just four plates, one for black and one for each of the three colors, red, blue, and yellow.

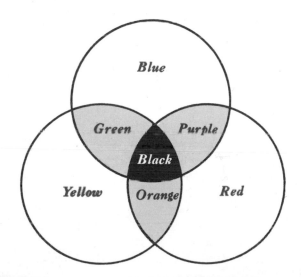

PRINTERS' PROGRESS

One reason why printing plays a more important part in our lives every year is that the printing industry keeps growing and improving all the time. When the first electric motor was invented, for example, printers quickly began to use this new kind of power for their presses, and this helped them do better and cheaper printing.

Two of the many recent inventions used by the printing industry are the electronic engraver and the phototypesetting machine.

An electronic engraving machine

This **electronic engraving machine** makes halftone engravings on plastic sheets by means of an electronic eye and a hot burning tool.

The operator fastens a photograph around one end of a cylinder and a sheet of plastic around the other end. Then he switches on the machine and the cylinder begins to turn around.

As the cylinder turns, the photograph passes beneath the electronic eye, which scans every tiny bit of its surface. The plastic sheet passes beneath the burning tool at the same time. When a dark portion of the photograph is beneath the eye, the electronic control makes the burning tool burn away the surface of the plastic

so as to leave large dots which will print dark on a printing press. When a light portion of the photograph passes beneath the eye, the electronic control makes the tool burn away the surface of the plastic so as to leave small dots which will print light on a printing press.

By eliminating complicated photography and messy acid etching, which take a great deal of time, this electronic engraver makes a halftone in a few minutes instead of several hours.

A more complicated model of this machine can separate a color photograph into the colors blue, yellow, and red, and quickly engrave the different color engravings necessary to print colored pictures.

A photo-typesetting machine

This **photo-typesetting machine** makes it possible to print words for reproduction by photo-offset or gravure presses without first setting metal type.

When the operator presses the keys, he fills a line with matrices, just as the operator of an ordinary type-casting machine does. But the matrices on this machine do not have raised letters which act as molds to form metal type. Instead the letter on each matrix is in the form of a stencil cut out of a tiny piece of film.

Each time a line is filled the operator presses a key and the first matrix in the row is lifted up into position opposite a beam of light. The light projects the image of the letter onto a strip of film in the special camera that is built into the machine. The film keeps moving, so that as the letters are projected onto it, one after the other, they appear on the film in neat rows.

When all the words in a story have been photographed in this way, the film is removed and developed.

Then it can be used for the preparation of the plates on a gravure or photo-offset press.

A calendering machine for smoothing paper

Paper for printing

Modern printers use hundreds of tons of paper every day, and good paper is necessary for a good printing job. But paper for printing is of many different kinds — thick and thin, rough and smooth, dull and glossy. And a printer must know which kind of paper is the best one to use for each printing process and for each job. If a Bible or a dictionary is printed on very thick paper, for example, it becomes such a big book that it is hard to pick up. That's why those two books are usually printed on very thin paper.

Newspapers are usually printed on a rather soft paper called **newsprint**. It is cheap, and that is one reason why it is used for the printing of papers that must sell for only a few cents each. Newsprint comes in big rolls that weigh three quarters of a ton

each. The world uses more than 12 million tons of newsprint every year, and the United States alone uses over half of that amount.

Most books are printed on paper that is tougher than newsprint, and that does not become brittle and yellowish when it gets old. That's why books ordinarily last longer than newspapers.

Paper for books usually comes in flat sheets of various sizes instead of on big rolls. Most of it has a dull surface. Sometimes the surface is rather rough, and then it is used only for the printing of fairly large type. If a printer tried to print tiny letters on rough paper, the bumps in the paper would break them up and they would be hard to read.

But the paper used for certain kinds of books and magazines has a smooth, shiny surface. It is called **coated stock** because it has been coated with certain minerals and chemicals to give it a glossy finish. It is especially good for the printing of photographs and full-color halftone pictures, and that's why picture magazines are often printed on this kind of paper. Very glossy paper is not good for the printing of type because the shiny surface seems to make the letters dance, and this is tiring to a reader's eyes. That's why the words of some books are printed on dull paper, and the pictures are printed on sheets of coated stock. Then the dull sheets and the glossy sheets are fastened together to make the finished book.

Paper-makers and ink-makers too work together with printers all the time, to make printed material handsomer and longer lasting and easier to read.

59

DID YOU KNOW

That the first books ever printed especially for the amusement of children were made by an English printer and bookseller named John Newbery about 200 years ago? Today in the United States alone about 1,300 different children's books are printed every year, and every year one of these books is chosen by the American Library Association for a special award called the Newbery Medal.

Mew, Mew, Mew

Bow, wow, wow.

That Braille is a system of printing for the blind, who have to feel letters instead of seeing them? Letters printed in Braille are formed of raised dots or points in special patterns. Each pattern stands for a letter. A pattern that looks like this ⠋ stands for the letter F, and a pattern that looks like this ⠗ stands for the letter R. This method of printing was invented by Louis Braille, a French teacher of the blind who died in 1852.

TAILOR RIDING A GOOSE.

Here you may see what's very rare,
  The world turn'd upside down;
A tree and castle in the air,
  A man walk on his crown.

60

That all United States stamps, bonds, and paper money are printed by the Bureau of Engraving and Printing of the government's Treasury Department? Postage stamps are printed at the rate of about six million a day in large sheets on big rotary presses that apply gum to one side of the paper and print designs on the other side. Dollar bills and other kinds of money are printed on flat-bed presses from steel engravings made by hand by skilled experts. All bills are printed on a special kind of paper which has tiny red and blue threads in it. This paper can't be imitated, and criminals who print counterfeit bills on other kinds of paper are usually caught and punished.

WORDS PRINTERS USE

case—a shallow tray divided into compartments and containing a font of type

chase—a strong metal frame into which a page of type and cuts is fastened

colophon—a printer's or publisher's trade-mark

cut—a photoengraving of a picture

font—a complete set of type in a particular style and size

form—a page of type and cuts locked into a chase

furniture—blocks of wood used in locking type into a form

galley—a metal tray filled with lines of type

galley proof—a printed copy of the lines of type in a galley

justifying—filling out a line of type with space bars to a specified length

mat—a papier maché copy of a page of type used to make a stereotype

matrix—a metal mold for making new pieces of type

plate—a rubber, metal, or plastic replica of a page of type and cuts which is put on a press and used for printing

point—a unit of measurement equal to 1-72 inch

quoins—pieces of metal used in locking type into forms

space bar—a blank piece of type used to separate one word from another

type metal—a mixture of lead, tin, and antimony used for making type

INDEX

The First Book of Printing • The First Book of Printing • The First Book of Printing •
k of Printing • The First Book of Printing • The First Book of Printing • The First Boo
The First Book of Printing • The First Book of Printing • The First Book of Printing •
k of Printing • The First Book of Printing • The First Book of Printing • The First Boo
The First Book of Printing • The First Book of Printing • The First Book of Printing •
k of Printing • The First Book of Printing • The First Book of Printing • The First Boo
The First Book of Printing • The First Book of Printing • The First Book of Printing •
k of Printing • The First Book of Printing • The First Book of Printing • The First Boo
The First Book of Printing • The First Book of Printing • The First Book of Printing •
k of Printing • The First Book of Printing • The First Book of Printing • The First Boo
The First Book of Printing • The First Book of Printing • The First Book of Printing •
k of Printing • The First Book of Printing • The First Book of Printing • The First Boo
The First Book of Printing • The First Book of Printing • The First Book of Printing •
k of Printing • The First Book of Printing • The First Book of Printing • The First Boo
The First Book of Printing • The First Book of Printing • The First Book of Printing •
k of Printing • The First Book of Printing • The First Book of Printing • The First Boo
The First Book of Printing • The First Book of Printing • The First Book of Printing •
k of Printing • The First Book of Printing • The First Book of Printing • The First Boo
The First Book of Printing • The First Book of Printing • The First Book of Printing •
k of Printing • The First Book of Printing • The First Book of Printing • The First Boo
The First Book of Printing • The First Book of Printing • The First Book of Printing •
k of Printing • The First Book of Printing • The First Book of Printing • The First Boo
The First Book of Printing • The First Book of Printing • The First Book of Printing •
k of Printing • The First Book of Printing • The First Book of Printing • The First Boo
The First Book of Printing • The First Book of Printing • The First Book of Printing •
k of Printing • The First Book of Printing • The First Book of Printing • The First Boo
The First Book of Printing • The First Book of Printing • The First Book of Printing •
k of Printing • The First Book of Printing • The First Book of Printing • The First Boo
The First Book of Printing • The First Book of Printing • The First Book of Printing •
k of Printing • The First Book of Printing • The First Book of Printing • The First Boo
The First Book of Printing • The First Book of Printing • The First Book of Printing •
k of Printing • The First Book of Printing • The First Book of Printing • The First Boo
The First Book of Printing • The First Book of Printing • The First Book of Printing •
k of Printing • The First Book of Printing • The First Book of Printing • The First Boo